A Moonchild's Heart

By: Bridgett Muckle

ISBN-13: 978-1-7352021-3-6

Editors: Tracy Brown

Cover Design: Bridgett Muckle

Illustrations: Bridgett and Joyce Muckle & Marquez Howard

To the sons and daughters of the moon and water. To everyone that cries from pain and beholds the beauty of life.

Follow my social media pages for more
Moonchild Moments.

Instagram: amoonchildsheart
Website: www.amoonchildsheart.com

Full Moon

Release, Lost, Pain

Static

A full moon watches over her child surrounded by darkness. She can't decipher an escape because she loves life here. A plot twist unravels in her mind as she floats on a cloud of possibility staring into the night's static. Moonchild, naked and never observed in her purest form. Void in her eyes, damaged skin, and scars exposed. On her knees but forgotten how to pray. The full moon will illuminate her path to restoration, and her purest form will heal the nations, but for now.....she's floating.

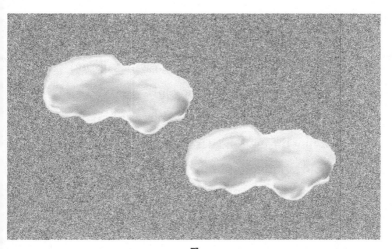

Heart vs. Head

My heart a fearless and adventurous child
willing to explore your darkness.
It's warm and comforting because
similar stories are inscribed on the soles of our feet so
we're walking into the same purpose.
The symbols across our knuckles identical so
we fight and survive the same.
Our scars indistinguishable from each other.
I only view you as a lover.

My head like a protective mother
giving our love a curfew, but
the streetlights came on hours ago.
My head discovers my heart high with you and
takes my heart to jail with no bail.
While detoxing, my heart becomes a fugitive
rampaging through the desert searching for your love.
My mind stumbles after the restless heart and wonders
when will the heart learn to stop repeating stories
hoping for alternate endings.

R.I.P

Your love like walking on hot coals that

cool in a bath of my tears.

Your love a dead end or venom that slowly kills.

Your heart a cemetery

I no longer live in.

Song

In the song of life,

why can't we just be?

Take vacations to our memories

so I can spend more time with you.

We'd be the note making the

song of life beautiful.

In the song of life,

time so fragile

while in this vessel.

Immortal beings living a mortal life, immorally.

Pretty faces shedding

humble beginnings, clarity, and loyalty.

Sometimes in the song of life

I'm the disturbing note.

The horrible ending.

Silence

Some abhor silence but today
we formed an alliance.
Silence.
She'll be my best friend and worst enemy.
Help me explore the inner me but
push me towards insanity.

Life After

I hated the bags under my eyes, so
you placed kisses underneath them.
"I see you and will never have eyes for another."
Those words still replay in my mind because
my bags slowly faded.
Was your kiss that magical?
Or did you just melt my stress away?
Now, tears comfort where your lips touched.
I didn't treasure the final kiss and
now, I'm blind without you.

Lost

Is love a constant state of mind

or a never-ending battle?

Sometimes I don't like my reflection in the mirror.

I don't love who I'm becoming.

Where did I lose myself?

Skeletons

In the land of the living,

many are dead longing for nourishing bread.

Starving as they feast on vices and insecurities

believing success comes from

climbing down the ladder of morality.

Disconnected from our bodies.

Declining calls from breakdowns

to chase the money.

Ego—the cause of death as

heartbreak causes sharp chest pains

secrets the size of boulders weigh on stomachs.

In the land of the living, many are dead as

skeletons resurrect from dark thoughts and

break out of closets searching for love again.

Within the chaos, the living and dead…

synonymous.

Communion

You poured into me.
Drunk off your words.
Nobody deemed me worthy
to pour into.

You broke bread with me.
I've never been fed before.
The bread—stale

My belly ached and vision blurry, so
I fasted from you.
But my feet returned to your table to
break stale bread.
How do you always find me?
Why do I always return?
Awakening to you.
Praying, for the day,
we will break fresh bread.

Night Sounds

Insomnia

I've been walking in the dark for hours.

Do you hear the train?

at least it has a destination

Do you hear the birds chirping?

at least they have a song to sing.

Do you hear the dog barking?

at least he is alert.

I don't know my destination.

Or have a song to sing.

Instead of being alert, I'm too trusting.

Lately, people contemplate I'm in pieces

based upon my decisions.

Judging my imperfections not

willing to make connections.

Their perception of me partly fantasy so

can you relieve my frustration?

Help me discover peace?

Because I can't sleep, and

I've been walking in darkness.

Deceit

You don't practice what you preach.

You're a false prophet.

A fake lover, and

I'm drinking your red Kool-Aid.

Departed from my expectations

to follow the smell of your fragrance.

Thinking I'm tasting love when it's

twisted truths...wasted time.

Your "pure intentions" misguided.

You only understand love as manipulation, and

I refuse to die in a man's arms that won't

kill his pride to observe my smile.

Confused

Are you attempting to win my heart again,

or play with my emotions?

You've done both before.

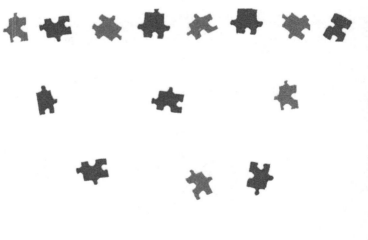

Embers

The fire in our bellies erupted last night
transforming our love to ashes.
We're dead to each other.
As I awaken, smoky hair seeps into my nostrils.
A lingering memory of our love
burning down last night.
Waking up alone
I no longer live to please you.
I allowed you to destroy the Goddess within.
You no longer live here.
Pieces of me left with you.
Your lease on my heart –expired.
Waking up to scattered embers in our…
My bedroom…my living room… my bathroom.
Looking into the mirror,
I realize what freedom feels like
a new beginning after the darkest
knight.

Masquerade

I feel enraged when stepping out of character.
You feel authentic when stepping outside of your
character because it's a role you play.
We are not the same!

Flame

Pulse pounds.

He's dying inside

Heart beats.

He ain't alive.

Smile bright but his inner light dim.

Losing energy, fading quickly.

Why you let them steal your fire?

Looking into those red eyes

I see a spark remains.

I'm your match, Let's connect and

set the world a flame.

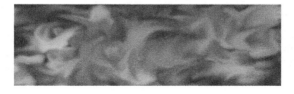

Trigger

Warning:

Trauma

Fireworks, on Independence Day,
echo flashbacks of wars
and losing friends while
fighting for a country
that never felt like a homeland.

The ice cream truck's song—
the soundtrack to his brother's blood
painting the concrete red
while their mother screams.

"Happy" the song playing when
walking into an abortion clinic,
so she won't observe the face of her rapist
when awakening in the morning.

Our ancestors whipped, beaten, sold, and murdered.
But the strength and royalty in our DNA outweighs
the trauma.

Déjà vu

Eye contact as
memories collide
and chills flow down your spine.
Flashbacks, reminiscing of a love like mine.
You're holding her hand, but
I hold your heart.
Now, she's standing in my place,
and she really owes me thanks.
Reaping all the benefits
of our long nights, my tears, and pain.
Reaping the harvest of the dreams
I planted in your mind.
When was the last time you felt alive?
When my heart ignited your power to love and thrive.
When was the last time you felt loved?
When I listened to the stories
of your scars and kissed them goodnight.
I'm still the only place you feel safe.

You're the only place I feel pain.

Our love can't remain, so

We look into each other's souls from afar and

Wave.

Cantrell

I've been screaming in private and
crying in public.
Conversing with the moon at midnight and
sleepwalking at daybreak.
Cutting my skin and split ends hoping everything
comes together.
Smiling and laughing in the faces
of my mother and lovers.
Taking 50 minute showers, then hiding under covers.
My pain in disguise and undercover but
now it's about to debut to
lackluster reviews of
"He doesn't have a reason to be sad or angry."
from people that don't know my story
or the thoughts running through my head on the daily.
People claiming I don't need therapy,
but I need something
besides liquor, blunts, and pussy.

I'm tired of Remy being my confidant and
kush being my sedative and
pussy my midday and midnight snack.
What do you do when you feel under attack?
But you're the only one who sees your enemy?
If I kill myself that'll be the first time you notice
Me.

Hollywood

Pour Henny to heal the scars.

Smoke loud to quite the pain.

Spilling my heart to my reflection

far from perfection.

The person I've been neglecting.

How'd I get here?

Face to face with my worst fear—myself.

Slowly becoming what disgusts me.

Caked on makeup, ass shots,

color contacts, and bleached skin.

Forgotten the beautiful girl within

no one to stitch the seams of my broken life.

So tonight

I pour Henny to heal my shattered dreams.

Smoke loud to quite the inner me.

This conversation stays between

me, myself, and I.

Condolences

Please keep your symphony of sorries
because your voice doesn't sound like her.
Keep your half-assed and hollow hugs
because your embrace doesn't compare.
Emptiness—the resounding emotion
so withhold "sweet" gestures because
you feel like a jester entertaining my sadness.
Entertaining my pain.

To Our Mother

We've allowed our greed and overindulgence
to spoil and rot your roots
while neglecting you amongst the chaos.
We destroy ourselves while watching you burn.
Production plants implant gases
as chemicals inhibit us to grow
Turning lungs to black coal.
The depths of your being filled with
waste that waves can't evict.
Disconnected—not observing our reflection in you.
I'm sorry we confused dominion with domination and
neglect to preserve and protect you.
My bare feet haven't touched grass,
visited sandy beaches, or run in the rain lately.
One day we'll whimper I'm sorry while
gasping for our last drop of air.

However, this is the consequence of rejecting a mother's love.
You'll place dead roses on our graves and shed tears of indifference.

Last Hours

"Let's go outside."

Air flows into her black lungs as

fresh cut grass and summer showers tease nostrils.

A cough reminds me of the inevitable.

Babies cry, birds chirp, cough more and more.

Death's four walls entrap my body, but

my soul wants to fly.

"Let's go home."

The drive bumpy and swerving.

Who's driving this dog gone car?

She grips the wheel with shaky hands.

Vertigo…my world spins.

Sky Blue. Wind blows. Flowers bloom.

Almost home.

"What's that on the radio?"

My child replies, "Someday We'll all be Free."

"Let's go inside."
A beautiful white house stands tall with
memories of cracking pecans and summersaults.
The screen door opens.
"Someone needs to clean up this damn mess!"
Too weak…
I'm picked up and taken to a warm bed
stabilized by the oxygen man as
catnaps shift day to night.
Sunday dinner is served, and
I know them collard greens don't taste like mine.
A younger version of myself hugs my neck and kisses
my cheeks.
They all express good-bye
as my breath continues to decrease.

"Let's rest."
The reaper man is coming.
Wait…my body convulses and shakes.

I'm already home. I don't wanna go.
Low sobs. A soothing touch. A soft voice echoes
"Momma, we gonna be alright."
I hear you my child.
Shaking stops. Low sobs. Transition.

Now, I'm home and
Someday We'll all be Free.

Full Moon Moment

Someone asked why I'm so distant.

Please talk to and blame the moon.

AND

You AND me.

The beginning of the end

uttered in those three words.

AND!......far more than a three letter word

separating

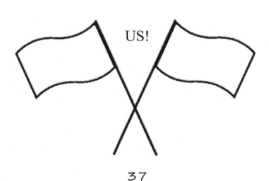

US!

Mahogany

Pride and prejudice produce wrinkles her warm and bright smile can't iron out; a jaw drops as the white coffee mug falls like an autumn leaf. Black coffee violently kisses the wooden floor when she stares at their intertwined fingers. She observes the undeniable essence of love in her grandson's eyes gazing at the beautiful girl. She scoffs with disgust then cracks a mischievous smile.

"Well, first she needs to sweep up this broken glass and then mop this coffee up."

Mahogany's smile transcends to wide eyes and a speechless expression.

Tears of anger well up in her eyes because his grandma can't decipher how love is color blind.

As tears fall, Mahogany storms out into the blazing sun. She'll never be good enough for her grandson. Chaos clouds her mind as the car accelerates over the bridge. Grant's shaky voice a never-ending record,

"I'm sorry, are you okay?" Mahogany blasts the radio as ambivalent emotions blend with melodious melodies as sweat drips down her forehead.

"Grant, roll down the window.!"
She sparks a cigarette as Grant accelerates the car into overdrive crossing the bridge entering her neighborhood and rolls down the window. He thought everybody changes with time as smoke permeates the atmosphere mixing with pine trees and tension.

"You will probably have black, tarry, and shriveled lungs from smoking so much."

"Well then my lungs resemble your grandmother's heart."

Mahogany gently blows the cigarette smoke in his direction. Grant slams on the brakes, snatches the cigarette from her mouth and throws it out the window.

"Don't talk about my grandmother like that!"

"Oh, but you allow her to disrespect me!"

Mahogany's fist repeatedly hits the dashboard until Grant grabs her arm and kisses her hand as she sobs.

"I'm tired of this shit, Grant!"

"Me too, your parents think I'm white trailer park trash!"

Nose to nose with Grant, Mahogany pinches both of their cheeks and states,

"Because all they want to see is this, but we understand each other's hearts"

Grant's glassy eyes jerk the car into drive repeating,

"They comprehend the past but not our future."

The '93 Buick whips into Mahogany's driveway. Grant looks at the immaculate, three-story, Southern-styled home and shakes his head.

"I'll call you later on." He exclaims.

Mahogany gazes as the Confederate flag license plate drives into the sunset and wishes her parents wouldn't take Grant's potential for granted and that coffee wasn't the only thing his grandmother liked black.

Keys

You still hold the key…to my heart.
I've changed the locks, but
you're a master locksmith
intruding and looting my love.

Losing

After losing you,

every death remains inferior.

Yes, I'm impartial.

You're my first love.

They don't love you like I do.

You'll always be present.

Never past tense.

More than heaven sent.

Still smell your scent.

Turn it into a fragrance, and

never let go.

Twenty-Five and Not Fine

Four friends are at a restaurant on Essence's birthday. They are at a vegan restaurant and finished eating and drinking several bottles of wine.

Essence: I don't know y'all I feel stuck like I should be further in life.

Unity: Girl, you are doing great! Don't do this on your birthday. You have a great job in your career field.

Essence: I hate that job. You all hear me complain about that shit daily.

Tahira: Hell yea we do!

Rubi: Look at where you stay! Your house renovations are amazing, and you have great roommates.

Essence: Rubi, my parents letting me rearrange my room aren't renovations

Rubi: Hey but you and Michael have been rocking for

a minute.

Essence: Girl, I don't know if that shit is going to last.

Rubi: okay well I'm done trying to cheer you up

Tahira: Well at least you alive.

Unity: And doing good with your vegan diet.

Essence: ehhhhhh I kind of went to Fatima's yesterday. I got a ten-piece half hot and half lemon pepper extra wet. It was a rough day at work.

Tahira: Damn, then why we at this vegan restaurant!!

Rubi: Well just focus on the fact you have great family and friends.

Tahira: That loves you!

Unity: And you're only 25!

Essence: I know I know, but I just feel stuck!! I just don't know my next move.

Knocking

Love— the essence flowing

through his bloodstream and

molded into his bone and marrow.

His love overflows so

he asks why am I so cold?

I pretend it's something in the air,

in my cup, or the moon.

Isn't it full?

I can't tell him the truth.

My tongue articulates hypnotizing lies.

I play charades while he plays zero games.

He raids my heart searching for my love for him

and turns up empty.

I make him the scapegoat as

he scrapes to preserve his love.

Wanting my eyes to look less mysterious and dark

I can't tell him that…I can't tell him

the heartbeat he hears at night are my skeletons

knocking.

my body he knows…like his own

My heart remains unknown

as the knocking of my skeletons send us to sleep one

last time.

Chandler

There is a church or liquor store on every street corner, and you chose the ladder combined with cocaine on occasion. I became tired but accustomed to your broken promises while waiting and looking out the window. I never hated an object so much in my life—the window. The window held and comforted me as I looked outside waiting. I wanted to completely shatter or throw black paint on it. However, those actions would only be a reflection of my heart since you're not around….shattered and dark. Did you think leaving and abandoning me made me a mythical being? A fabrication of your imagination? Like if I wasn't in front of your face, I wasn't real. Well I've been around the sun 25 times without you. Every year it's better but emptier. Even though I survived without you, my world is still smaller.

A Moonchild's Heart : Full Moon

I hate and love having a telepathic relationship with you. I felt you missing me, and I replied with loving vibes for you to visit. My reflection in the window waited with me as disappointment became a familiar friend. I felt when you were drunk and high. I cried myself to sleep for two weeks, and not even my sister's comfort stopped the tears. I felt your despair, euphoria, your trapped mind, and spirit. I remember feeling when your soul left this earth. I was in Vegas, during spring break, and just experienced the best orgasm of my life. Then, this uncontrollable wave of sadness commenced to rush through my body. Death and all your sins choked me until tears fell from my eyes in Sin City while the sun started to rise. Almost like I tasted the cocaine that transitioned you from life to eternity.

As I stood over your casket my blood boiled. The first time I remember meeting you was in a casket. Your old pictures did you justice even though you allowed that poison to destroy our family and your vessel. Surprisingly, on the outside, you were still handsome. The resemblance within our facial features evident and uncanny. I look just like you. People say I act just like you, and I fucking hate that! Afterwards, I stood in the church across from the liquor store wishing you'd choose me. Would you do it differently if granted another chance? Was chasing a high better than loving your daughter? Regardless of your answer, I will love and forgive you.....someday.

Question

4 years until I'm 30......Can someone please point me in the direction to financial security?

Pearl

To the women that never put their feet up because
they're constantly hitting the pavement,
wiping sweat from brows and tears from eyes.
To women with full plates but never being served.
To women with aching, stiff backs, and broken hearts.
To women planting seeds and
using that harvest to feed the hungry.
Isn't your stomach growling for nourishment too?
Don't you need someone feeding your soul?
Aren't you a woman that needs
rest, love, and good food?
You're a beautiful pearl.
Refined and regal but
life is your wasteland
instead of your oyster.
To all the women
the world will continue spinning while
you recover from the vertigo of life.

You aren't created to be strong all the time.

You're a beautiful pearl so

wear your confidence around your neck and

Rest.

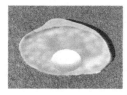

Casual

Your touch empty.

Your kiss hollow.

We're both shallow.

An oxymoron.

Longing for closeness

but yet so far   away

come over?

Omw!

You up?

Wyd?

Interlude to Lt.

Love reluctant to search for me because
I'm living in a simulation of love.
Hoping I'll awaken to feel love between us
in our covers,
our conversation,
and our embrace.
In actuality,
We've carried this lust to full-term and birthed
a non-committed relationship
with subliminal messages
of care and complacency.
Your heart and mind conflicted so you're speechless.
While I'm searching for "love"
in the place we first met and
where we last kissed.
Cupid reluctant to shoot his finally arrow
because I'm confused if you're my "beau."

Searching for a love that feels like home and
not extended stay or rent to own.
A love that feels like
Saturday morning cartoons then
cleaning all afternoon.
A love that feels like
Sunday dinner at Big momma's house.
A love that leaves me with zero questions and
never leaves me alone.

Christina

He grabbed the back of my neck and
pulled me closer.
Eye to eye.
I still refused to see the deceit.
Nose to nose, but
I couldn't smell his rotten intentions.
Mouth to mouth he said,
"You really irritate me, but
I do care about you.
We fight but sometimes
That's what friends do."
In the next moment, he kissed me.
As I kissed him, I thought
How are friends and a kiss in the same sentence?
Why am I allowing myself to be here again?

Wayward

Some men act like they're God's gift to earth,
but unable to birth life.
Ladies, beware!
Don't let men fertilize what
they neglect to nourish with
consistency, communication, and effort.
Stop looking for words to validate what
his actions already solidified.

Ladies be aware!
Sometimes you're following
traumatic tendencies instead of your heart.
Returning to similar cycles with different people.
He won't discover clarity in your eyes,
nor should you desire for him to.
He'll distort your vision while
inhibiting you from achieving your
vision. Be aware

Trigger Warning:

Cassie and Mr. High-five

Mr. High-Five observes me stumble in my friend's apartment
quarter past nine already tipsy and high.
His friend hollers, "Smash!"
Mr. High-five smacks his hand.
The night grows older, the drinks get stronger and colder.
My vulnerability lower and his persistence higher.
Mr. High-Five waits outside my friend's bedroom.
I cling to the floor for refuge
as my friend states, "You can't sleep here."

Mr. High-Five blocks the front doorway.
He doesn't walk me to my dorm but
encourages me to stay.
Pretending to sleep, I ignore his voice repeatedly echoing,
"Why don't you come over to this couch?"

His persistence irritating so I give in.
Even with the space between us,
He touches my thigh and kisses my neck.
As he drops my panties, I cringe
"Get on top" he says
Is this how it's supposed to feel?
What am I supposed to do?
It doesn't hurt as bad as people said
why is he making loud ass noises?
My high left...reality set in
I stop and lay back down.
He reaches for me, but
I quickly jerk away with tears boiling down my face.

While walking to my dorm in the morning,
Mr. High-Five states, "Let's do it again sometime."
I'm confused about it.
What does he think happened last night?
Does he think I was playing hard to get?

A Moonchild's Heart: Full Moon

This shit is fucking with my mental

Far from consensual, but he doesn't understand.

With a smile on his face, I wave good-bye to Mr.

High-Five.

Invisible

Invisible…
No attachment. No strings.
My low eyes and tears startling but
let me be in peace.
I'm releasing as I wander
receiving counsel from my mother.
She consoles and speaks words
that return me to sanity.
Invisible....
Exploring the rabbit hole alone
instead of shouting out.
Don't want a caring soul around.
I rather listen to the thunder's roaring pain
or the tree's fears of abusive winds and rotting roots.
I rather ask the raindrops
why they taste acidic?
Ask the flower why she's wilting.

A Moonchild's Heart: Full Moon

I'll express that I feel the same.

My roots are distorted and destroyed as

life's winds force me to bend.

A sweet kiss turned to acidic poison

as my heart still burns for his lips.

I'm not sweet anymore

since people constantly pick and

consume my kindness to feed their greed

and emotional needs.

I'm slowly dying...becoming invisible.

Invisible, but I like it.

Invisible long enough to understand.

Then, I'll travel the dirt road home and be

Invincible!

Quote #1

"Bridgett needs to look out for Bridgett. Think for yourself."

— Dad

Insert your name for Bridgett

Bridgett's Full Moon Outro

Daydreaming with the moon

plotting on tomorrow while drinking moonshine.

In time, I won't resemble a broken compass, and

the taste of adventure won't spoil

after touching my lips.

These phases leave me floating, growing, and restless.

I'm finding it harder to be happy and funny.

Life is clowning me while smothering my spirit

I'm confused and wondering.

Why am I not following my heart?

Wandering with all the answers….

Can you tell me which way to go?

As I take another shot,

here's to hoping my tomorrows

look better than my current mind state.

Writing this to complete my pain because

in the end…in the present I'm already dead.

Fear

The sun sets over our honeymoon bliss.

Now, tensions rise with the sun.

Arms caressing my body now suffocating

instead of comforting.

Stiff expressions and stale words at breakfast

as coffee brews neglecting the issue that

I don't believe your words anymore.

Questioning every consonant and vowel.

You've been lying to me!

Unable to live without

my racing mind and rapid heartbeat.

Contemplating your next manipulation tactic as

You feel me drifting.

Occupying the dark crevices of my mind for too long.

Eating away at my happiness,

spontaneity, and serenity.

You're restraining me from stories

the moon christened me to fulfill.

So, fear you are released!

I've packed your things because

my dreams are too tempting

not to taste, not to chase

breaking free from your chains.

Until

As women we love
completely, freely, and fiercely
but sometimes
for too long.
Focus deterred when
men are our epicenter
shaken by their every move
whether ill intent or genuine.
So, until love doesn't mirror losing myself
until love doesn't mirror captivity
until love doesn't mirror war

I'm alone.

Full Moon Prayer

Please keep my spirit protected and free as I discover myself while drawing near to you. Let the darkness come close enough to lead to my healing. Strengthen me in my weary moments and restore peace to my chaotic mind. In this moment, let my fear and anxieties dissolve as I release my lack of boundaries to the midnight air. Under this full moon, I set fire to negative thoughts that constantly echo in my mind. I drown the expectations for others to rescue me from myself and solely depend on the universe for soul guidance. Underneath this full moon, I am enough, and I am anew.

Amen

Story

If we accept the narrative before us,

we will never write our own story

even though we think it's our own.

Anew

What do you need to commit to ashes?

What's blocking your passion?

Who and what needs a eulogy?

After the ashes settle,

your new beginning awaits.

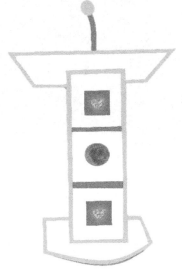

New Moon

Create, Infinite, Love

Clarity

A new moon watches over her child surrounded by light and walking in her purpose. Knowing she's worth it. Bouncy curls, bright smile, spirit freed, dancing in the streets and floating high off life. Manifestations transitioned possibility to prosperity. Moonchild, naked in her purest form, with a sparkle in her eyes, skin moisturized, trauma and scars healed. On her knees, before her altar, giving thanksgiving and praise to the ancestors for staying faithful during her foolishness and fearfulness. The new moon illuminates her path. This journey not easy, but she decides to be the author of her life, and nobody will steal her crown.

Kaleidoscope Rapture

Lost in the purple lilac of the night
lost in your pink morning sky
enamored with the kaleidoscope of life.
Presently, live is beautiful
with an energy of abundance and peace.
Amnesia to the past
ghost and darkness no longer haunt me.
The future—a pleasant dream.
In this rapture, you take me higher
closer to God.

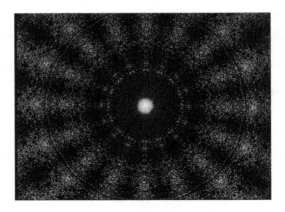

Ocean

As I dive into you, we become one.
I'm formless, limitless, and timeless
when sharing our energy, I'm light.
Present but observe the future in your eyes.
The world serenely intensifies as
chilling clarity flows down my spine.
I've loved you since catching fireflies and
running through sprinklers in the summertime.
Waltzing with you as you fall from the night sky.
here our connection strengthens.
I feel the strongest here with you.
I've never wondered what language the ocean speaks.
The ebb and flow of your waves need no translation.
The depths of your wisdom speak to my soul.
I will sit on different sandy beaches and listen
to the secrets of your heart and stories of your past.
You're eternally seeing the emotional turmoil and
harboring the pain and souls of my people.
I feel you both at shore as the

high tide massages my feet.

The ocean's language majestic stillness and resilience.

Always moving in purpose as mortals sleep and

Everything I long to be.

In the waves, resides peace, passion, and salvation.

Mystical

Our wombs—powerful portals.

All women are oracles.

Intuition enhances our foresight

making our words prophetic.

Ancestral knowledge and strength within our bones.

Their presence in the atmosphere and

the air we breathe.

We're created to thrive as spirit guides us.

More than magical...

We are oracles.

Self

Hug yourself when disappointment strikes,

and your reflection is blurry.

Cry to mourn pieces of you

yet to return.

Heal scars you never inflicted.

Create boundaries for manipulative spirits.

You're valuable without lovers validating your

existence.

Please, forgive yourself!

Self-love is unlearning the self-hatred America

teaches.

Self-love—a never ending battle

until it transforms to a consistent state of mind

and continually repeats.

Self-love—a forever evolution

forever revolution.

Flame

Fire is Fire.

We decide if it destroys

or refines

as we stand in the flames.

Collete

What do you do when society hates your complexion and family tolerates your existence? Is it my fault my skin is black? Is it my fault my mother never loved...after my father? Is it my fault she never called me beautiful? My mother's heart broke, when I was born, not because of my tears but because I survived the delivery. Is it my fault when she gazes into my eyes the reflection of my father and her mother push her mind off the cliff of sanity? I wanted to save her. But how can you be someone's savior when they view you as a devil?

So I hit the road. Since the age of 16 I've been alone searching for a place better than here. In my mind, Heaven was a myth! A fairytale land that I'd wear a disguise to invade because my life's resume doesn't meet Heaven's requirements. That's the main reason I never committed suicide because I don't know what's on the other side of death. I once heard an old lady state, "Death comes in threes." Well, my mind, body, and soul deceased the day I met Cole or rather the old Collete died. I found Heaven and my authentic self-looking into Cole's eyes. He deciphered my unspoken words no one cared to translate. On that summer day, I discovered Heaven isn't a myth nor a destination in the sky but within people roaming this earth.

"What are you looking at?" were the first words I spoke to him. The gates of Heaven opened and replied,

"The pain is all over your face." I never knew my darkness and pain radiated from my face, but now I felt it seeping from my pores. I was exposed, but my first taste of freedom came within that same moment.

"Well, you can't do shit about it."

"But I'd like to," Cole smiled and expressed.

Those words. Those words awakened my untouched heart strings, and I continued to let him play them because every stroke....every stroke felt divine...like healing. So vulnerable, I told him everything about my miserable past and felt whole for the first time in my life. I thought Cole was in love with my pain.

After a while, he'd look at my wholeness with disgust and venture to another dysfunction leaving me unable to function. Leaving me ready to jump off the cliff of sanity that he helped me find footing on. Those were the dark thoughts that ran through my mind at night when he wasn't by my side. However, Cole proved with time his timelessness. I fell in love the moment he said,

"I'll still crown you my queen even if you believe your mother's heart broke when you were crowning from her womb."

Before Cole, I only interacted with hellish people; maybe the demon my mother observed in me was within her. However, none of that matters now because I've seen, felt, tasted, and breathed Heaven.

WORDS

The sound of your voice combats stagnancy.

Words break the chains of bondage as syllables slide

off tongues

and consonants conjure new visions.

In one breath, your words release and create energy

that the universe longs to hear.

She longs to hear your pain, gratitude, and aspirations.

What's the point of love if you don't express it?

What's the point of gratitude without thanksgiving?

Conversations with the universe usher you into

a sanctuary of revelations, peace, and understanding.

Soon your words will make

water dance, cast out demons,

birth legacies, and lead rebellions.

When words touch the realm of reality,

their magic heightens

creating nightmares or dreams.

Do you know whose breath flows through you?

Whose blood pumps through your veins?

If so, speak!

Don't surrender by hiding your voice
in this world war of words. As
your words discover movement,
I pray you follow their lead.

Soulmate

Slamming on failing brakes as I crash into you, but

I like this. Far from an accident more like

divine intervention at the intersection

of fantasy and reality

Unexpected but destined.

Creation

Let your imagination run wild on me and
the canvas of my body be your fantasy.
I sit on your throne, and you're unable to speak.
Worshipping me as you savor my flavor.
Let me taste your lips.
Then, we create a masterpiece as you enter paradise
where you explore every angle.
We create love when our lips touch.
The rhythm of our heartbeats collide and intertwine
creating the baseline.
Accompanied by the slapping
of your hands against my ass.
My screams resounding like a cymbal and
a symbol of our love.
Our love smooth as Jazz,
explicit as Hip Hop
chill as Reggae.
As we make love,
We create music...we create life.

Power

We give our power away daily
saying yes instead of no
saying no instead of yes.
Embracing what we should run from
running from what we should embrace
allowing emotional phases
to transition into an eternal state.
So I'll sleep under moonlight to restore my strength
while cuddling discernment
as the rain waters my intuition and
cleanses my spirit.

528Hz

The earth revolves at love's frequency.

We discard our humanity, birthing destruction,

when rejecting love.

We destroy ourselves when neglecting love.

Love—our core weeping for recognition

like a malnourished child.

Frightened by her sacredness

some never explore love's frequency, but

can we throw away

What we're created from?

What we're ignorant of?

At times, love feels elusive, but

one can't embody what isn't nourished.

At times, love feels elusive but its presence

In the breath of your lungs and

The soil of the earth.

Love—indispensable since we're infinite

God is love and we're molded in Her image.

She sustains our life and rests in love. While

earth revolves at love's frequency,
we're in tune with the chaos.

Stars

Backbone strengthens

voice exudes grace

walk embodies confidence.

Stepping into the star's appointed path

Safe Place

Him: Where is your home?

Her: Some days I have none other days plenty.

Him: Can I be one when you have none?

Her: What about the days when I have plenty?"

Him: Hopefully, you'll choose me.

BTF

Nobody loves quite like you.

We speak the same love language but

obtain diverse dialects.

Heart ache hidden

within your past love stories.

Your love language I can't decipher,

but I'll sit with you for hours within days,

days within months,

months within years to become fluent in your love.

Can I be your second language?

I want to be fluent in your sarcasm

comprehend your unspoken words

know your visions like they're sown in my womb.

Love never truly alludes us because it's our core.

We must dive deep within ourselves

to discover its power.

All I ask as we dive, you'll

Be Bold

Transparent and

Free.

Rubi and Sapphire (Part 2)

She walks past, and my heart speaks before my mind can stop. "Rubi!" My boyfriend's head turns as her surprised smile of recognition brought relief.

Good, I think internally, she remembers my face. Thank God I don't look like some weirdo, and this is the first time I seen her smile. It's beautiful.

"Passion! Never thought I'd see you again."

Damn, I think, She doesn't remember who I am.

"Passion?" I reply.

"Uhh Yea, when we met at the football stadium you had super cute passion twist. I didn't get your name so when my friend asked who was that I just said Passion, and now I'm rambling. This is awkward."

I laugh, "Nah you're good! But my actual name is Sapphire." As another awkward unconscious gesture, I extend my hand. When she shakes my hand it happens again. The first time her eyes captivated and washed away my anger, but this time her touch evaporates my nervousness. How is she having this effect on me? Is this mutual?

"Well your actual name is just as pretty."

I smile, "Thanks, Rubi this is Marcus...Marcus this is Rubi."

"What's up!" My boyfriend says.

"Nice to meet you. Well, I'll let you two get back to dinner."

My heart wants to blurt out join us, but my mouth doesn't utter the words. Marcus and I watch her walk away, and I wonder w*hy didn't I introduce him as my boyfriend?* However, he doesn't care as he snatches the last shrimp off my plate...

"So your girlfriend seems nice." He snickers as I roll my eyes.

"I barely know her."

"Okay...Passion" Marcus burst out laughing as I throw a fry in his face.

"I'm going to start calling you that."

"You better not!" Marcus places a kiss on my lips. I enjoy the moment even though I know it won't last.

Intimacy

Lovers that never made love.

Reached a level of intimacy lost in eternity.

They don't understand...not on our frequency.

Scared of the sacred only scratching

the surface of mediocrity.

Manifest

I love you! You're a part of my inner being.
When you caress my body,
I feel anew so smooth as
our souls infuse
never feel used.
You are my peace. You feel like home.
Time slows down for us.
Please, come quench my thirst because
I received visions of us before my eyes met your smile
and your hand touched my skin.
When we kissed our past lives
together intoxicated my mind.
You teach me it's never too soon to love again.
So why waste time?
You don't feed my doubts and insecurities
Do small things to make my heart sing.
Heart and intuition scream yes so
I will love you until our sunsets.

Queendom

Alone, I'm strong.

Yes, I'm hardworking;

I rule my own kingdom.

No man will steal land from under my feet, or

My destiny written before creation.

I promised my ancestors

that I won't spit on their graves

by delving in wicked ways

that don't feed my soul.

But you feed my mind.

The angels sing our praises when we're together

because you're a king.

A King wakes me up in the morning

and cooks breakfast

A King makes me moan as I pour ecstasy

onto his taste buds

and will supply the seed to bring our angel into being.

A King will take our daughter, Amora, to choir

practice one day.

This isn't blasphemy because

when I look in your eyes

That's all I see… a King.

A piece of heaven

A piece of God in your eyes.

The most high made us in Her image

So who are you?

Yes, I'm hardworking ruled my own kingdom

Until a king transformed it into an Empire

Our seed will continue the dynasty.

Quote #2

"How's your heart, mind, and soul?"

—Mom

Rubi and Sapphire (Part 3)

Meeting Rubi at the restaurant in Atlanta I attempt to shake off as a coincidence. However, as I walk into the sex store in New York I realize destiny either envisions different plans for us or loves toying with my emotions.

"Are you stalking me?" I ask Rubi as I walk up to the counter.

"I could ask you the same thing. You walked into my workplace. I'm here interning for a law firm and work nights here."

"Okayyyy a lawyer...nice!"

"So what are you doing here?" Rubi asks.

"I mean it's a sex store....kind of obvious."

"No, I meant in New York."

"Oh my mother lives here, and she's been sick so I'm staying with her for a few weeks."

"Oh, I'm sorry Sapphire!"

"Don't say sorry. I hate when people say that about family shit."

"Because you think it's a knee jerk rather than genuine?"

"Yea," I utter in surprise, "uh….I'm going to look around the store."

Rubi comes from behind the counter.

"So what are you looking for here? Whips, restraints, ball gag?"

"Woah," I throw my hands up, "Just the basics...a vibrator."

Rubi starts walking over to the section.

"Welp vibrators are far from basic nowadays."

My eyes widen as I look at all the possible options.

"So do you want your boyfriend to use it on you because we have this…."

"Nah", I quickly interject, "We broke up awhile back...creative differences."

"Oh"

The bell rings as an older couple walks into the store. Rubi turns around,

"Hello welcome to Pussy Power Sex Store. I'll be right with you."

"I'll let you look around," she states, "I'm here if you need anything."

I glance at the wall for two minutes and snatch the first vibrator that looks like it'll make me nut at least three times and walk towards the desk.

"Damn, that was quick" She laughs.

Rubi walks behind the counter to ring up the vibrator.

"Do you want to go out tonight?" Rubi asks.

"Yea sounds cool I've never been out in New York before'"

"A virgin to New York night life. Trust me you'll love it, but I'm limiting you to 3 drinks. Can't have you stumbling like at the football game.

"Hey that's one extra drink than the limit I set for myself so we're good."

Rubi laughs as she hands me the bag.

"Just come back here at midnight"

"Isn't that a little early for a sex store to close?" I ask.

Well, people can go to the Pussy Poppin Sex Shop up the street because Pussy Power has to close so this pussy can pop!"

My eyes widen, "Well I'll just watch because I can't do all of that."

"I'll teach you don't worry," Rubi winks at me.

"Okay see you at 12."

In that moment walking out of the store, I felt this is potentially the greatest love story, or a Lifetime movie waiting to happen. Either way an adventure awaits.

Writer's Block

Never articulate I have writer's block. Instead, say my creativity is transmuting to other areas of my life. She will come back to my mind and pen with many stories and adventures to tell. I anticipate her return to learn more about the person I see in the mirror every day.

Hello

She says good morning to the flowers and birds and
good night to the moon after dancing with it.
Hugs the trees and cuddles with the grass.
People think she's peculiar but
Nature the singular entity
that remains consistent for her.
The trees always standing firm and strong and
the birds consistently sing their song.
The prickly grass—warm and comforting.
The moon a confidant as they exchange stories
about new changes and phases.
No, she's not peculiar but
observes the simplistic harmony and
humanity in everything
and it's infinitely there anticipating her conversation
and cold embrace.

107

The Break

P.S I have the power…now

My sacred heart won't grace your hands again.

I reclaimed my heart and ran.

Blood streamed down my stomach and thigh.

The world spun as I stumbled.

"My feet won't return to your table."

An epiphany followed me into the darkness that

my body is being purged of you.

I received new dreams.

The protection of angels and ancestors surrounded as

I regained consciousness and crawled to freedom.

New Moon Moment

Someone asked why I'm so free
Please talk to and blame the moon.

Love Letter to Pen

What's up with the sun, moon, and stars?
Lately I've been in emotional ruins
displaying my emotional beauty.
I know I'm a sensitive soul so
the fire in my belly burns a little differently.
My joy and rage hard to translate
so tears the unspoken language
of my pain and happiness.
In this moment, I'm relieved you've returned.
I'm lonely when you leave me.
I search for you in the night
and pray for you in the morning, but
You allude my presence.
It's been a minute since my heart spilled on paper, or
my soul cried out with ink or led.
You always find me in moments
I least expect or detect
You're my confidant soaking up my emotions and
Repeating every word back for deeper clarity.

Metamorphosis

Emotions create pathways to
self-discovery and recovery.
"You're too emotional and sensitive" they echo.
However, my metamorphosis is occurring while
They are complacent with being a caterpillar.
Afraid of isolation to secure their elevation.

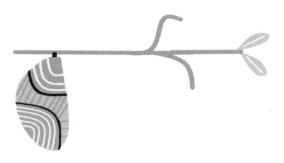

Cantrell

Tunnel vision full of demons
with no light at the end
because I'm the light!
As I delve deeper,
It shines brighter!
My demons attempt to worship me, but
I give them flowers as thanks and
banish them to the dark places of my mind
that's now a little brighter because
I am light!

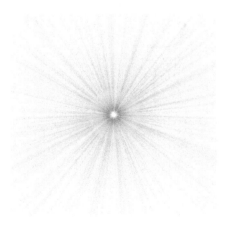

Spring

Some people you outgrow

I'm blooming while

You are still discovering your roots.

Regrets

Regrets = none

I poured into him without hesitation

So when he returns for a refill

There is nothing left to give.

The Whispering Spring

A free flowing and endless portal of possibility.
Premonitions while present.
I'm drinking from a reservoir of knowledge
sent by the ones who walked this
earthly plane before me.
The Whispering Spring—formless.
Always flowing through me
purifying and illuminating my destiny
while purging energies fighting to extinguish me.
Sustaining my sanity through whispers sent in the
wind and confirmation supplied by angels.
The Whispering Spring—a protector.
Springing into action to shield my heart
that's ever changing like seasons
Spring to summer
Summer to fall
Sometimes falling victim to ego
Not adhering to you.

The Whispering Spring—an ultimate enlightenment.

Never stagnant, reeking of pollution or ill intentions.

Always flowing, clear, and guiding me to eternity.

SHIP

To late night conversations filled with tears and
early morning adventures surrounded by nature.

The honey that makes life sweeter.

The salt of the earth sometimes making it bitter.

As angel and demons' debate at crossroads

our hands intertwine.

No matter the storm's turbulence

friendship remains

the waves and lighthouse

beckoning me to shore.

ART

The most handsome piece of art.
Who made you...this way?
I want to study you.
Your mentality, physicality, but
especially your heart.
It's so open!
I stumbled upon you broken, but
As we traveled to sandy beaches,
hiked to waterfalls, and
led line dances at summer BBQs
I've learned...I've learned
knives pierced your heart as
lovers rejoiced in its final beat.
Lovers dropped your glass heart, stepped on the
shattered pieces, and cried about
you making them bleed.
In cannibalistic fashion, lovers,
with watering taste buds
bit your heart dying to taste real love.

You should be dead inside but
you're here with me.
Now, with open hearts and no inhibitions
the possibilities are endless.

Vessel

You are a vessel of uncharted, endless,
and infinite possibilities.
Let only those that love and support you pour into
your vessel.

Extension

Created from the same supernova.

Vibrating on a similar frequency

falling at the same intensity.

You're an extension of me.

I embedded unfinished love lyrics in your heart

That continually run through your mind.

As we draw closer, the finished lyrics

appear on my inner thigh.

I'm an extension of you.

Your melanin the melatonin allowing

my anxieties to sleep.

My voice the antidote to your rage.

Your touch a cloak of peace under the stars

as you name constellations in my name.

Eyes powerful and gentle like the ocean we're beside

as we dive deeper and drift further.

Midnight walks on the beach transition

to an alcoholic drink.

The breeze is the angels approving our union—warm

and enlightening.

We are an extension of each other.

As we drink Henny and roll blunts

longer than extension cords.

Hopefully, one day you'll cut the cord

extending from our child.

Our souls are old friends on a new adventure.

If you believe in love after life,

let's spend our next lifetime together because

You're an extension of me eternally.

Stain-glass

The warmth and light shines on my body
the gentlest alarm clock.
As birds' chirp, my eyes open to
my lover's heart reflected and
projected on our bedroom wall.
Colliding colors dancing together
Blue, red, pink, green, yellow, orange, and indigo.
Colors that hold stories and secrets I've explored and
now I desire to worship her more.
Honestly, I'm speechless at the elegance
within the chaos.
The resilience within the pain
life within the death.
At the depths, her heart remains pure.
I'm waking up to a reality I dreamt years ago.
As I turn to kiss my lover,
The light of her spirit shines
through her stain-glass heart.

Note to You

Love your reflection more and
lust after adventure and purpose
ignoring every diversion that inhibits your creation.
Discover balance between helping others and
healing yourself.
Stop living life for others, and
redefine yourself daily.
More than extraordinary!
Stronger than your mind comprehends
with an unbreakable spirit.
You are worthy!
Please don't endure pain
to alleviate people's burdens that
hold their ego closer
than you.

I've discovered dimensions within
shed many skins that
people hold as evidence.
Alluding freedom's call
the only crime committed.

The Harvest

We yearn to observe the harvest quickly

comprehending the potential beauty.

Patience and presence!

The keys that unlocks growth and serenity.

We planted the seeds but

worry about it blossoming.

Are you focused?

On watering the seeds destroying

the weeds?

Being rooted in LOVE?

Being rooted in presence?

One day the crops will arrive

Harvest time because

we arrived here by being…here.

Horizon

When past lovers leave,
A deeper organic love searches for you
during the day as grass grows
under moonlight as the wind whispers.
Love is on the horizon.
Drawing closer with every passing morning and hour.
As my glow reflects off mirrors
Catching my eyes, I realize
"I am my greatest love."
"I will be my greatest lover" and
So will you!

Bridgett's New Moon Outro

I've found an oasis of escape
that isn't embedded in another's smile, touch, or hug.
Paradise after a purgatory between
peace and depression.
finding and losing myself.
I turned pain into creation after
tiring of being a safety net when I'm the catch.
Tired of auditioning for roles in the lives of
mothers, friends, and lovers when I'm the star.
You can't save everyone.
People neglect restoration because
they desire to live in the
debris of their brokenness.
Some people refuse to love again because
pain remains their companion.
Dressing it up in suits, ties, or ball gowns
claiming it's humorous and charming.
It's astounding from my pain I birthed you.
A paradise of escape I've spoken into existence.

A place where hummingbirds, dragonflies, and
butterflies convene for lunch.
Wind chimes play and the trees sway, so
I know angels and ancestors reside here.
I pray my land of milk and honey never spoils.
I'm finally at peace and
Found a home...within.

Eternal

This lifetime a shooting star
unexpected, beautiful, and quick
so don't contemplate what ifs.
Live in the fullness of your purpose
live in the fullness of you.

.

About the Author

Bridgett Loutrella Muckle was born July 1st 1993 and began writing around the age of 7. Recently, she graduated from the University of Georgia with a Master's in Social Work, and she currently resides in The Classic City. *A Moonchild's Heart* is her first work of poetry and short stories.